W9-BQS-640

Foods of Iran

Barbara Sheen

KIDHAVEN PRESS

An imprint of Thomson Gale, a part of The Thomson Corporation

THOMSON

GALE

Detroit • New York • San Francisco • San Diego • New Haven, Conn. • Waterville, Maine • London • Munich

© 2006 by KidHaven Press. KidHaven Press is an imprint of The Gale Group, Inc., a division of Thomson Learning, Inc.

KidHaven™ and Thomson Learning™ are trademarks used herein under license.

For more information, contact
KidHaven Press
27500 Drake Rd.
Farmington Hills, MI 48331-3535
Or you can visit our Internet site at http://www.gale.com

LIBRARY OF CONGRESS CATALOGING-IN-PUBLICATION DATA

Sheen, Barbara.
   Foods of Iran / by Barbara Sheen.
      p. cm. -- (Taste of culture)
   Includes bibliographical references and index.
   ISBN 0-7377-3453-1 (hard cover : alk. paper) 1. Cookery, Iranian—Juvenile literature. 2. Iran—Social life and customs—Juvenile literature. I. Title. II. Series.
   TX725.I7S445 2006
   641.5955—dc22
                                                                       2005022356

Contents

Chapter 1
Ancient Ingredients 4

Chapter 2
Welcoming Dishes 16

Chapter 3
Afternoon Treats 28

Chapter 4
Special Foods for
Special Occasions 41

Metric Conversions 53

Notes 54

Glossary 56

For Further Exploration 58

Index 60

Picture Credits 63

About the Author 64

Ancient Ingredients

Iranian food is one of the oldest cuisines in the world. For more than 3,000 years, Iranian cooks have depended on three ingredients—rice, lamb, and fruit—to create elegant, fragrant, and delicious dishes.

A Most Honored Food

Rice holds a place of honor in Iranian cooking. Iranians love the snow-white grain. It has been the mainstay of their cooking since the 4th century B.C., when **Silk Road** traders brought it to ancient **Persia** (the name for Iran until the 20th century) from India.

Not just any rice will do. Iranians prefer a rare type of **basmati** (boss MA tee) **rice** grown in northern Iran. Its

4

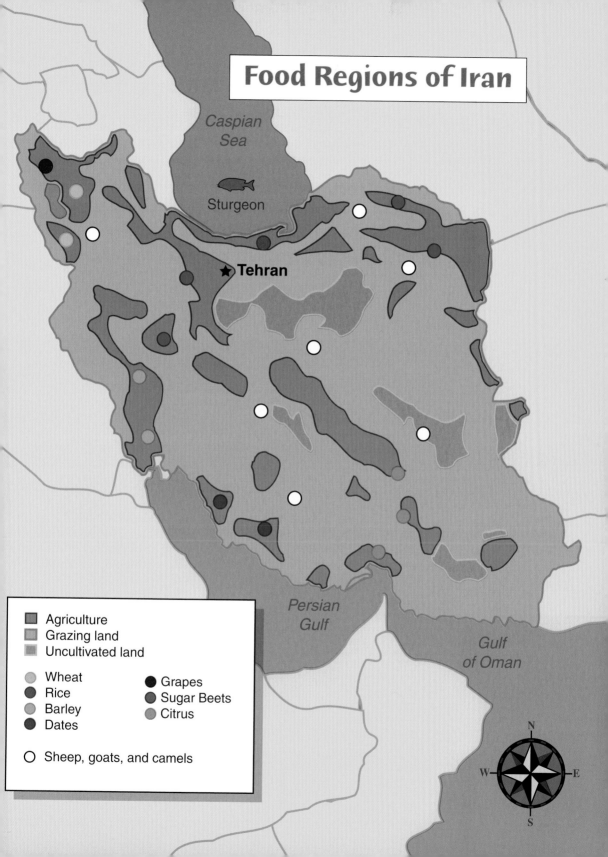

Food Regions of Iran

Caspian Sea

Sturgeon

★ **Tehran**

Persian Gulf

Gulf of Oman

Agriculture
Grazing land
Uncultivated land

Wheat   Grapes
Rice   Sugar Beets
Barley   Citrus
Dates

○ Sheep, goats, and camels

N
W — E
S

long, pointed, black-tipped grains have a flowerlike fragrance. Because it grows only in northern Iran, this rice is quite expensive, costing more than twice as much as rice grown in Southeast Asia.

Choosing such a precious product is serious business. Every year after the rice harvest, Iranians visit rice merchants from whom they purchase a year's supply of the grain. Because only the best will do, buyers carefully inspect the rice's color, length, and aroma before making a selection.

An open-air produce market provides many of the ingredients for Iran's flavorful cuisine.

Newly purchased rice is stored in a cool, dark place. But first, it is sifted through a strainer to remove any broken grains. These are saved for use in soups and stews.

The best grains are used to make **chelow** (che LOW), a fluffy white mound of steamed rice that is the centerpiece of almost every meal. It is often served on a glistening brass tray accompanied by grilled lamb. Sometimes meat, fruit, and vegetables are arranged in alternating layers with chelow. This is known as **polow** (po LOW), a dish from which Western rice pilaf—a mixture of rice, vegetables, and sometimes meat—originated.

Iranian cooks take great pride in their ability to prepare chelow. Each grain must be light, dry, and fluffy. A crisp golden crust known as **tah dig** (tah DEEG) must form at the bottom of the pan. "If you want to consider yourself a Persian cook," advise experts at the *Persian Mirror,* an Internet magazine dedicated to Iranian culture, "the first thing you need to do is to learn how to make rice."[1]

Cooking Rice

This is not an easy process. First, Iranian cooks soak rice overnight in salt water. The salt firms the rice, which keeps it from falling apart during cooking. Then the rice is strained and placed in a pot of boiling salt water. After about ten minutes, the rice is strained again and, to keep the grains from sticking together, it is tossed with a fork. Next, the cook melts butter in a saucepan, spoons the rice on top in a pyramid-like

At harvest time, workers painstakingly separate red saffron strands from the bright purple flowers.

shape, and sprinkles **clarified butter** and **saffron**, a rare golden spice, over the rice tower. This gives the rice a rich flavor and an intoxicating aroma. Finally, a clean dish towel is placed over the rice and the pan is covered. The rice is left to steam for about 30 minutes. The dish towel absorbs any excess moisture, which keeps the rice from getting soggy.

When the rice is done, the cook fluffs it and piles it onto a serving tray in a delicious pyramid. The tah dig is scraped from the pan and served separately as a crisp, buttery treat. The results are worth the effort. It is

Chelow

Iranians are very particular about their rice. Any long-grain rice can be used, but Iranians prefer basmati rice.

Ingredients:

3 cups long-grain rice
6 tablespoons salt
⅔ cup melted butter
½ teaspoon saffron dissolved in 2 tablespoons
  hot water (optional)

Instructions:

1. Soak the rice in salt water over night. Drain the rice.
2. Bring a pot of water with 6 tablespoons of salt to a boil. Add the rice and boil for 10 minutes.
3. Remove and drain the rice. Pour half of the butter into a saucepan. Spoon in the rice to form a pyramid shape.
4. Place a clean dish towel or a double layer of paper towel over the pan and cover the pan firmly with a lid. Cook over medium heat for 25 minutes.
5. Remove the pot from the stove and allow to cool for 5 minutes. Be careful opening the lid, since hot steam will be produced.
6. Pour the rest of the melted butter over the rice. Sprinkle with liquid saffron.

Serves 4–6

rice, according to Iranian chef Margaret Shaida, "at its most refined and sophisticated—light, fragrant and wonderfully digestible, each separate grain so light and airy that a spoon is provided with which to eat it."[2]

Chelow is often served with lamb, which is the most popular meat in Iran. This is because most Iranians are Muslims, many of whom follow strict dietary rules that forbid the eating of pork. Beef is permitted but beef is scarce because it is difficult to raise cattle in Iran's dry desert and mountainous terrain. Sheep, on the other hand, thrive here. Because Iranians raise fat-tailed sheep, which store all their body fat in their long tails, the meat is never fatty. It is lean and tender, and the tail makes an aromatic cooking fat.

Many Lamb Dishes

Iranians have been raising sheep since around 9000 B.C. Over the centuries, they have developed a large variety of lamb dishes. They pair the buttery-soft meat with a wide range of contrasting flavors. For instance, they may stew it with fruit and beans, bake it with prunes and potatoes, layer it with herbs in polow, sauté it with split peas and yogurt, or mix it with onions to make giant meatballs. They grill it on skewers, combine it with rice, and pack the mix into vegetables or fill casseroles with it. They roast whole lambs and stuff them with nuts and fruits, then they use the bones to make hearty soups. These are just a few of lamb's uses. According to Shaida, "For those of us familiar with roast lamb, lamb

Herds of sheep are a common sight in a nation that prides itself on its many lamb dishes.

chops, and lamb stew, the many inspired and exotic methods of preparing sheep meat come as a revelation. . . . From waferlike grilled **kebabs** and creamy meat-based porridges to stews, roasts, and dumplings, the range is as sweeping as it is sophisticated."[3]

Fruit

Fruit is another important and ancient part of Iranian cooking. In fact, Xenophon, a 4th-century-B.C. Greek philosopher, wrote an article praising the fruit he was served when he visited Persia.

Back then, Persian shepherds and soldiers carried dried fruits with them when they left home. The fruits

Fresh Fruit Cocktail

Fresh fruit cocktail is a popular Iranian dessert. Seasonal fruits are used, so the recipe can vary depending on what is available.

Ingredients:
1 tablespoon orange juice
1 tablespoon lime juice
2 tablespoons sugar
1 cantaloupe, cut into small chunks or balls
¼ cup seedless grapes, cleaned
¼ cup strawberries, cleaned and sliced
1 peach, sliced
3 fresh mint leaves, chopped (optional)

Instructions:
1. Combine the orange juice, lime juice, and sugar.
2. Put the fruit in a pretty bowl. Pour the juice over the fruit and mix gently.
3. Cover the dish and refrigerate for one hour.
4. Sprinkle mint leaves on top before serving, if desired.

Serves 4–6

were portable and did not spoil easily, and their high sugar content provided quick energy. Today, dried and fresh fruits such as apricots, dates, figs, and melons are used to make syrups, preserves, sherbets, and ice cream. They are also eaten for snacks and desserts and are always offered to guests. Travel experts at Iran Tour, a travel agency devoted mostly to Iran, explain: "If you ever eat at an Iranian

A shopper picks through ripe pomegranates in a Tehran marketplace. The deep red seeds of the fruit (above) make a tangy syrup.

Edible Flowers

Flowers play an important role in Iranian cooking. They add a sweet perfume to Iranian dishes. The crocus is probably the most important flower in Iran. Saffron, the most widely used spice in the country, comes from the crocus flower. It takes about one acre of crocuses to produce 1 pound (.45kg) of the spice, which is why it costs more than $400 per pound. But since a little goes a long way, Iranian chefs do not worry about the price.

Rose petals are less expensive, but also important. They are often sprinkled on chicken to sweeten and scent the dish. Dried rose petals are often made into fragrant jams. Rosewater, a liquid made with distilled water and rose petals, is drizzled on chelow and added to many Iranian sweets. And many ice cream vendors sell rosewater ice cream and ices.

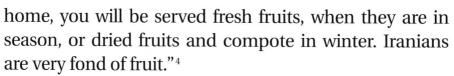

home, you will be served fresh fruits, when they are in season, or dried fruits and compote in winter. Iranians are very fond of fruit."[4]

Sweet fruits are not the only fruit popular in Iran. Iranians adore sour fruit. They add a hint of tartness and a fresh fragrance to soups, stews, and casseroles. A favorite is the dark red pomegranate. Its juice is made into tangy syrup that is combined with ground walnuts, onions, cinnamon, and lamb to create a stew called **fesenjan** (fes en JOON). Its zesty flavor is so beloved by Iranians that, according to chef Nesta Ramazani, "the ultimate test of a cook's ability in Persia is the quality of the fesenjan he or she can prepare."[5]

Tiny green sour grapes, cherries, and tamarinds, which look like dates but have a salty-sour taste, are also popular flavorings. So are quinces, tart fruits that resemble pears. Barberries, which are too sour to eat fresh, are dried and layered in polow or stuffed into roasted lamb.

Dried Limes

Dried limes are another popular treat. The sight of the bright green fruit drying in the sun is common in Iran. Used whole or ground into a powder, dried limes add a sharp citrusy flavor to stews, and tickle the taste buds of diners who eat them sliced with their meals. Iranians say the sour flavor refreshes them.

Indeed, the fresh taste of sour fruits, the beauty of perfectly cooked rice, and the melt-in-your-mouth tenderness of lamb give Iranian cooking delicacy and elegance. It is no wonder Iranian cooks have depended on these ingredients for thousands of years.

Welcoming Dishes

Hospitality is an important part of Iranian culture. It is not unusual for unexpected guests to drop in at mealtime. Iranian cooks do not mind at all. There is always plenty of Iran's favorite dishes—stews, soups, and kebabs—to go around.

The Mainstay of Iranian Cooking

Stew, or **khoresh** (chor ESH), is the mainstay of Iranian cooking. At any time of day, in any kitchen in Iran, you are likely to find a pot of khoresh bubbling on the stove. Filled with herbs, fresh and dried fruits, beans, vegetables, and a small amount of lamb, chicken, or fish, khoresh is far and away the most popular dish in Iran.

Whether at home or in a restaurant, Iranians frequently enjoy a meal of stew, rice, flatbread, and tea.

Khoresh with Green Beans

Khoresh is a tasty stew. This recipe calls for lamb, but any stew meat or sliced chicken can be used.

Ingredients:

2 onions, peeled and sliced thin
cooking oil
1 pound lamb cut into 1-inch cubes
3 cups hot water
½ teaspoon each of salt, pepper, and cinnamon
1 pound frozen green beans
2 tablespoons tomato paste
1 tomato, cut into small pieces
2 tablespoons fresh lemon juice

Instructions:

1. Fry the onions in oil until they are golden. Add the meat and cook until it browns.

2. Pour hot water over the mixture, then add the salt, pepper, and cinnamon. Reduce heat to low, cover, and let the mixture simmer for 45 minutes.
3. Add the beans, tomato paste, tomato, and lemon juice to the mix. Simmer for 1 hour.
4. Serve over rice or with warm bread.

Serves 6

Only the freshest ingredients are used to make khoresh, so the herbs, vegetables, and fruits change with the seasons. That may be why there are so many different varieties of the stew. Split pea and lamb khoresh, for example, is one popular choice. In ancient times, the lamb used in this stew was precooked and preserved in oil. Today, it is made with fresh meat, yellow split peas, onions, and dried limes, which give it a hearty flavor. Rhubarb khoresh, with its mix of red rhubarb and green mint, is another favorite. It is as colorful as it is tasty.

Herb khoresh is perhaps the most popular khoresh of all. It is made of onions, lamb, dried limes, kidney beans, and a mix of fresh herbs. Its fresh taste and mouthwatering aroma is beloved by Iranians. According to Shaida, "An Iranian man is the envy of all his friends and neighbors when his wife can produce the perfect ghormeh sabzi [herb khoresh]."[6]

Common Elements

Although the ingredients differ, all Iranian stews have a number of things in common. They are all cooked slowly, which allows plenty of time for the flavors to blend together. They all have a slightly sour taste. And they all contain onions.

Onions have always been an important part of Iranian cooking. In fact, many historians think that the first wild onions originated in Iran. Ancient Persian stew recipes all contained onions. The difference between ancient stews

A steaming bowl of lamb and white bean stew, topped with fresh herbs, makes a hearty meal.

and modern khoresh is that today, the onions are fried before they are put into the khoresh.

Fried onions not only add a delicious scent and flavor to khoresh, they thicken the sauce to just the right consistency—neither too thick nor too thin. This is very important, because when khoresh is served, the sauce is poured over chelow. Then the meat is piled in the center of the sauce-covered rice. The results are so scrumptious that whether for family meals or as a way to welcome guests, khoresh is almost always on the menu.

A Bowl of Friendship

Soup is also common in Iranian meals. In Iran, sharing soup is a way to show friendship. Soup is always offered to guests. Iranian chef Najmieh Batmanglij explains: "Soup plays a vital role in Iranian tradition. . . . Sharing a bowl of soup is believed to forge the bonds of friendship. . . . Sometimes, friends or lovers sip from the same spoon to seal their devotion."[7]

Iranian soup is known as **ash** (awsh). Ash is a thick, fragrant soup made with herbs and beans. It is a meal in itself. Because ash is so vital to Iranian cooking, an Iranian cook is called an ash-paz.

Like khoresh, ash is simmered for hours. It is usually cooked in a glistening copper pot. The pot's heavy

Promise Soup

Promise soup is a special Iranian soup that contains a wide variety of ingredients. Iranians say it helps prayers to be answered. These prayers usually concern the recovery of a sick loved one.

Friends, neighbors, and the family of the sick person supply the ingredients, which are cooked in one pot. Everyone helps to make the soup, and everyone eats it. If the prayers are answered, the loved ones of the sick person promise to make the soup every year and serve it to the poor.

weight and composition allow the heat to be distributed evenly. As a result, the ingredients cook well and taste wonderful.

The variety of ash that Iranians make is endless. One 16th-century Persian cookbook contains 50 different ash recipes. Modern favorites include carrot and cabbage ash, spinach and split pea ash, and bean and noodle ash. Fruit ash, made with dried apricots, barberries, prunes, raisins, beans, and onions, is another top choice. Fragrant herbs and spices enrich every type of ash. **Garnishes** such as sliced onions and ground cinnamon add to the soup's taste, aroma, and beauty.

Adding Meat

When meaty lamb bones are added to the ash, it is called **ab-goosht** (ahb GOOSHT). Cooking the meat in the soup gives the broth a rich flavor. Iranians do not serve the soup with the meat in it. Instead, they remove it, and the vegetables too. The meatless broth is served with fresh, hot flat bread. The meat and vegetables are pounded into a thick paste, which is topped with fried onions and served either as a side dish with the soup or as a separate meal. Because ab-goosht is delicious and can serve as two distinct meals, it is popular with rich and poor Iranians alike.

The National Dish

Kebabs, meat threaded on skewers and grilled over a charcoal fire, are another Iranian favorite. Roasting meat on sticks over an open fire is one of the oldest forms of cooking. Iranians have been making kebabs in much the same way since the 7th century A.D. In fact, Iran's national dish is chelow kebab, or lamb kebab and rice.

Iranian flat bread, hot out of the oven, accompanies many favorite dishes.

A home style restaurant in central Iran grills skewered kebabs over a hot charcoal fire.

Iranian cooks make dozens of different types of kebabs. Lamb fillet, lamb liver, lamb heart, ground lamb, and chicken kebabs are popular. All are made in the same way. First, the cook **marinates** the meat overnight in a mixture of herbs and grated onions mixed with lime juice or yogurt. The acid in the marinating liquid makes the already tender meat as soft as butter.

When the meat is ready for cooking, the cook threads it onto a metal skewer that is about 9 inches (23cm) long. A piece of fat-filled lamb tail is placed between every two pieces of meat. When the meat cooks, fat drips from the bit of tail onto the meat, moistening it.

To ensure that the meat cooks evenly and does not slip off the skewer, the cook matches the width of the skewer to the type of meat being cooked. The smallest skewers, which are ⅛ inch (0.20cm) wide, are perfect for chicken and liver. Lamb fillet is placed on ⅜-inch skewers

The Sofreh

In the past, Iranian families dined around the sofreh (so FRAY), a colorful tablecloth embroidered with poems and prayers that was spread on the floor over a Persian rug. Diners sat cross-legged around the cloth and ate food with their fingers. A piece of flat bread was often used as a plate. Although some rural Iranians still eat in this manner today, most modern Iranians eat at a traditional table, sit on chairs, and use plates, forks, and spoons. But a sofreh is still placed on the table, and families still gather around it to enjoy a good meal.

An Iranian family eats in the traditional style, seated cross-legged around a cloth spread on the floor.

(0.97cm), and ground meat fits well on the widest, 1-inch skewers (2.54cm). Once this is done, the skewer is placed over a hot charcoal fire, where it is turned around and around. As the meat turns, it is brushed with a mixture of

Lamb Kebab

Kebabs are not difficult to make. You will need metal skewers to cook the meat. This recipe calls for lamb, but beef can be used as a substitute.

Ingredients:
1 onion, peeled and chopped
½ cup lime juice
½ teaspoon each of salt and pepper
1 pound lamb, cut into 2-inch cubes

Instructions:
1. Combine the onion, lime juice, and salt and pepper.
2. Place the meat into the mix and marinate it in the refrigerator for at least 1 hour.
3. Thread the meat onto the skewers.
4. Grill the meat on a grill or in a broiler. Let the meat brown on one side, then turn the skewers over. The meat is done when it is brown on both sides.
5. Remove meat from the skewers before serving. Serve with hot bread or rice.

Serves 4

lime juice, saffron, and butter. The charcoal fire and the cooking meat fill the air with a mouthwatering aroma.

Serving Kebabs

Finally, when the meat is brown on the outside and pink and juicy inside, it is ready to eat. The cook removes the succulent meat from the skewers and piles it onto a platter. It may be accompanied by hot, flaky flat bread that diners wrap around the juicy bits of meat. Or it may be served beside a huge platter of chelow dotted with saffron and melted butter. The results are so delectable that after an especially memorable chelow kebab dinner, author Setareh Sabety noted: "This kabob [kebab] and that perfect rice that accompanied it made the earth move under my feet. I ate this simple yet noble piece of my heritage with humility and quiet gratitude."[8]

With hot, tender kebabs, mouthwatering soups, and richly flavored stews all piled high on Iranian tables, it is no wonder that guests love to drop in at mealtime. These favorite dishes are hard to resist.

Afternoon Treats

Iranians typically enjoy a snack in the afternoon. They usually eat pastries accompanied by sweet, hot tea or unique cold drinks. The same drinks and sweets are kept on hand to greet visitors and guests. "You could stop by to pick up a book from your neighbor's house," quips Iranian humorist Hamid Taghavi, "and you're instantly dragged inside and are told to eat goodies."[9] Favorite goodies include **baklava** (baagh la VAH), nut cookies, **sharbat** (shar BAHT), and **doogh** (doog).

Baklava

Baklava is a delicate, feather-light pastry that Iranians have been snacking on for thousands of years. Scholars say it originated in Assyria in the 8th century B.C. and was brought to Persia by Assyrian traders shortly thereafter. It is made of paper-thin layers of sweet, flaky dough filled with nuts and honey, and topped with rose-scented syrup. Because the dough is only about ⅓ inch (0.84cm) thick, it is quite difficult to make without tearing it. Although some Iranian bakers make their own baklava dough, many buy sheets of premade dough known as **phyllo** (FI-low).

To make baklava, bakers place one or two phyllo sheets in a baking pan coated with butter. Then they cover the dough with a layer of filling. The filling is covered with another sheet of dough, and so on.

Baklava comes in different shapes but most varieties are made with nuts, honey, and sweet, flaky dough.

Iranian bakers fill baklava with ground almonds and pistachios mixed with honey and a hint of ginger. Iranians have been growing pistachios since 7000 B.C. Today, Iran is the world's leading producer of pistachios, and many people say the Iranian variety is the best in the world. They give the pastry a delicate buttery flavor.

Almonds are also plentiful in Iran. The almonds used to make baklava are often stored in tins filled with fresh flower petals. The almonds absorb the flowery scent and perfume the pastry.

A shop owner, surrounded by bags of pistachio nuts, awaits customers.

Rolled, layered, and filled pastries of all sorts are decoratively displayed in a pastry shop window.

Iranian bakers do not mix the two nuts together, but instead spread them in alternating layers. The pistachios, which are pale green when shelled, form a green layer, while the almond layer is tan. This makes the baklava colorful and pretty. And because the final layer of dough is topped with syrup made from sugar, water, and two tablespoons of rosewater, the pastry smells divine. The result, which is cut into perfect diamond-shaped pieces, is sugary sweet, feathery light, and deliciously scented. Ramazani explains: "An elderly neighbor of mine called this pastry the 'food of the Gods.' It deserves the praise."[10]

Ancient Cookies

Nut cookies are another yummy accompaniment to afternoon tea. Iranians have been enjoying them for centuries. In fact, historians say that the ancient Persians were the first people to bake with sugar. Baking sugary nut cookies has been an Iranian tradition for more than 2,000 years. Indeed, the ancient Greek historian

Walnut Cookies

These tasty cookies are easy to make.

Ingredients:
5 egg yolks
¾ cup sugar
½ teaspoon cinnamon
½ teaspoon vanilla extract
2 cups chopped walnuts

Instructions:
1. Preheat the oven to 300° F.
2. Beat the egg yolks, sugar, cinnamon, and vanilla together. Add the walnuts and mix well.
3. Grease a cookie sheet. Drop batter onto the cookie sheet one teaspoonful at a time. The cookies should be about 2 inches apart.
4. Bake for 20 minutes. Let the cookies cool before eating.

Makes 20 cookies

Herodotus was served these delicious treats when he visited Persia around 500 B.C.

Besides their delicate flavor, what makes these cookies special is their composition. Unlike most cookies, these cookies are made without flour. The dough is made of eggs, sugar, and grated nuts.

Pistachios

The type of nut used depends on the cookie. Pistachio, almond, walnut, and coconut are all popular. Different flavorings, which are added to the dough, are carefully chosen to complement the particular nut. For instance, vanilla sweetens and scents walnut cookies, while rosewater and cardamom, a cinnamon-like spice, add a pleasant fragrance and flavor to almond cookies.

The small, round, golden cookies are often decorated with ground pistachios to give them color. Sometimes they are rolled in powdered sugar. They taste similar to a macaroon, so sweet and soft they melt in your mouth.

Ice-Cold Refreshers

When the weather heats up and Iranians crave an ice-cold drink to accompany their afternoon snack or to serve to visitors, they satisfy their thirst with sharbat or doogh. These are two of Iran's favorite beverages.

Ice-cold sharbat provides welcome refreshment on a hot summer day.

Sharbat is a mix of fruit syrup and ice similar to the treat Americans know as snow cones or slushes. Originally made with snow and served to important guests, sharbat is an ancient refreshment. Shah Tahmasp, a 16th-century Persian ruler, ordered his cook to welcome a European visitor in this way: "Let him drink fine sherbets [sharbat] of lemon and rosewater, cooled with snow."[11]

Ancient visitors to Persia were so taken with sharbat that similar treats soon became popular in Europe.

Tea Drinking

Iranians love to drink tea. They brew it in Russian kettles called samovars and drink it from tiny clear glasses. Since the glasses do not have handles, it takes practice holding them because they are so hot.

Iranian tea is quite strong. Iranians pour only a small amount of tea into the bottom of a teacup and fill the rest of the cup with boiling water. Milk is never added to the tea, but they do use sugar. Instead of putting sugar directly into their cup, they put a lump of sugar on their tongues and sip the tea through it.

Seated in a tea house, two men enjoy a cup of tea.

Ta'arof

Iranians are famous for their hospitality. As soon as a guest enters an Iranian home or office, he or she is offered tea and cookies. It is customary for the guest to decline the offer of food. The host or hostess then offers the food again, and the guest again refuses. It is considered polite to refuse the food three times before graciously accepting it. This custom is known as ta'arof (tah ah ROAF).

Modern iced desserts such as sorbet and sherbet began as sharbat. According to food experts, fruit flavored sodas have the same origin.

Today, sharbat is made of crushed ice and a wide array of syrups. Cooks create the syrups by combining fresh fruit juice, sugar, and water, and boiling the mixture until a sticky syrup forms. Popular flavors include orange, lemon, lime, sour cherry, quince, crab apple, rhubarb, and mint and vinegar. The last is extremely popular and is often taken along on picnics, since it is an excellent thirst quencher.

Sharbat is usually served in a tall, frosty glass. Some cooks add rosewater to the syrup to perfume the iced treat. No matter the ingredients, sharbat is not as sweet as American-style iced drinks. Instead, it has a tartness that Iranians love. According to Shaida, these "wondrous blends and balances of fruit syrups and ice quench the thirst in a most refreshing way. . . . Poured over ice, diluted with water and served in a tall frosty glass, they are an elegant reminder of traditional Persian hospitality."[12]

Healthy Treats

Sharbat is not only refreshing, it is also nutritious. Made from fresh fruit, sharbat is loaded with disease-fighting vitamins. This may be why Iranians often give sick family members sharbat.

Rich sour yogurt, used in drinks and other dishes, has been part of the Iranian diet for thousands of years.

Doogh is also used to treat sickness. This favorite Iranian drink is made with rich sour yogurt. Yogurt is full of essential nutrients and contains live bacteria that help keep the digestive tract healthy. So it is not surprising that Iranians not only drink the refreshing beverage for enjoyment, but also use it to treat upset stomachs.

Doogh is made with yogurt, salt, mint, and carbonated water. It is the most popular soft drink in Iran. Many Iranians use store-bought yogurt. Others make their own yogurt, just as their ancestors have done since at least 6000 B.C. To do this, they combine a starter culture of harmless bacteria with hot milk. The mixture is kept warm until the bacteria cause the milk to sour, thicken, and become yogurt.

Ready-made doogh is also sold everywhere, just like sodas are sold in North America. Although doogh is fizzy like American sodas, that is where the resem-

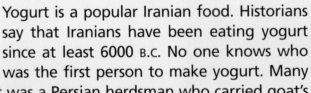

Yogurt

Yogurt is a popular Iranian food. Historians say that Iranians have been eating yogurt since at least 6000 B.C. No one knows who was the first person to make yogurt. Many experts think it was a Persian herdsman who carried goat's or sheep's milk with him in a sheepskin sack. The milk came in contact with harmless bacteria. The desert heat caused the mix to sour, thicken, and became yogurt. The ancient Persians liked the taste—and the idea that they could preserve extra milk by allowing it to turn into yogurt.

Doogh

This refreshing drink is very easy to make.

Ingredients:
8 tablespoons plain yogurt
1⅓ cup club soda, seltzer, or
    carbonated mineral water
¼ teaspoon salt
2 mint leaves

Instructions:
1. Combine the yogurt, club soda, and salt in a blender and mix.
2. Fill 2 glasses with ice. Pour half the doogh into each glass. Top each glass with a mint leaf.

Serves 2

blance ends. Doogh is not sweet. It has a salty, sour taste and a minty freshness. Iranians say there is no better way to cope with Iran's blistering summer heat, which can top 110° F (43°C), than with a cold glass of doogh. That may be why Iranians have been drinking the tart beverage for centuries. Experts at Salam Iran, a Web site dedicated to Iranian culture, explain: "For generations, Iranians have served yogurt as a soft drink in summer. . . . They dilute it with water, add a pinch of salt, spearmint, and call it abdugh [doogh]. Iranians, particularly in rural areas, keep the abdugh on hand and serve it to their family and guests on hot summer days."[13]

Whether it's a refreshing glass of doogh or sharbat, a plateful of rich nut cookies, or a sweet, flaky piece of baklava, Iranians and their guests enjoy their afternoon snack. The delicious taste of these treats is irresistible.

Chapter 4

Special Foods for Special Occasions

Iranians love to entertain. Special occasions give them a chance to welcome friends and family and to share special foods. Dishes such as jeweled rice, **ajil** (ah JEEL), and herb **kuku** (koo KOO) help make festive events more memorable.

The King of Iranian Dishes

Jeweled rice is often called the King of Iranian Dishes. This eye-catching dish starts with bright, golden, saffron-coated rice to which orange peels, carrots, raisins, butter, crystallized sugar, tart barberries, slivered almonds, and pistachios are added. The array of different colors is dazzling. The effect is not unlike a treasure chest

A plate of sweet, zesty jeweled rice is a delight at any meal.

filled with glittering coins and bright sparkling gems, which is how the dish got its name.

Jeweled rice is not only beautiful to look at, it also tastes and smells wonderful. It is often topped with rose petals. Their fragrance combines with the rich scent of saffron, the fresh fragrance of fruit, and the sweet smell of sugar to create a perfume suitable for a king or queen. But it is the taste of this remarkable concoction that is its crowning jewel. It is sweet, light, and zesty.

Jeweled rice accompanied by saffron-spiced chicken is a part of almost every festive occasion. It has been the traditional centerpiece at Iranian weddings for more than 1,400 years. To make its appearance even more dramatic, it is often served in a glistening edible bowl made of spun sugar. Its sweetness promises the newly-weds a happy life and its many jewels promise them wealth. No wonder food experts at the cooking Web

In Tehran's Grand Bazaar a nut seller displays his goods. Nuts are a special treat at New Year's celebrations.

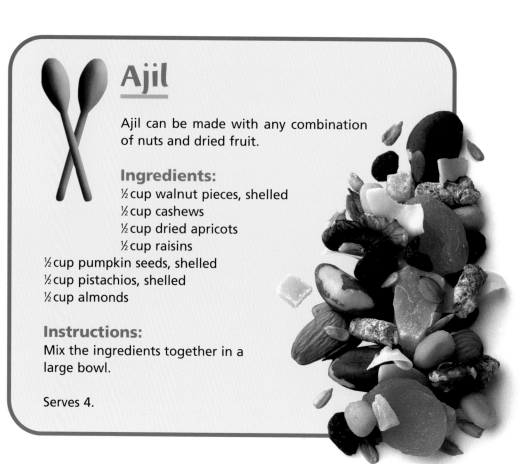

Ajil

Ajil can be made with any combination of nuts and dried fruit.

Ingredients:
½ cup walnut pieces, shelled
½ cup cashews
½ cup dried apricots
½ cup raisins
½ cup pumpkin seeds, shelled
½ cup pistachios, shelled
½ cup almonds

Instructions:
Mix the ingredients together in a large bowl.

Serves 4.

site Epicurious.com call jeweled rice "one of the glories of Persian cuisine."[14]

A Delicious Mix

In **Farsi**, the language spoken in Iran, the word ajil means "nuts." There are plenty of nuts, seeds, and dried fruits in the festive dish also known as ajil. It is served during **No Rooz** (No Rose), the twelve-day Iranian New Year's celebration, which occurs in the spring.

Before the festivities begin, shops throughout Iran are packed with large barrels brimming with dried fruits and nuts. There are apricots, figs, dates, cherries, peaches, raisins, and mulberries. Many have a tasty surprise in their center, where a crunchy almond has been substituted for the pit.

Almonds, cashews, pistachios, walnuts, hazelnuts, and sunflower, watermelon, and pumpkin seeds fill other barrels. Vendors freshly roast the nuts and seeds and sprinkle them with a little salt. The scent perfumes the busy streets. Holiday shoppers cannot help but buy a little extra to nibble on as they go on their way. Shaida explains: "The aroma of roasting nuts hauls people into fruit and nut shops by their noses. No one can resist a handful of hot salted nuts."[15]

There is no specific recipe for ajil. Cooks use whatever combination of nuts, fruits, and seeds they prefer. For instance, if a saltier flavor is desired, ajil may consist of almonds, pistachios, walnuts, hazelnuts, watermelon seeds, pumpkin seeds, and raisins. More dried fruits are used for a sweeter mix.

Some people buy ready-made ajil. During No Rooz, ajil comes in colorful boxes filled with a beautiful arrangement of nuts and fruits. Such boxes are popular holiday gifts.

Lucky Seven

No matter how varied the ingredients, one thing is constant—ajil always contains seven ingredients. This is because Iranians believe seven is a lucky number. According to Iranian tradition, if a person has good luck during No Rooz, he or she will be lucky in the coming

A family gathers for a traditional celebration of No Rooz, the Iranian New Year.

year. That is why hosts and hostesses offer ajil to No Rooz visitors, and visitors bring boxes of ajil to their loved ones. Sharing it is a way to wish each other good luck. And because nuts resemble little coins, eating ajil is said to bring wealth in the days ahead.

That is not the only reason ajil is popular. Eating ajil on the last Wednesday of the year is said to make people's problems go away, allowing Iranians to start the New Year with a clean slate.

Of course, it is doubtful that eating ajil can make a person's problems disappear. But ajil's yummy taste makes the No Rooz celebration more fun.

An All-Occasion Omelet

Herb kuku, a delicious omelet-like dish, is another New Year's specialty. Iranians make dozens of different types of kukus. The main ingredient in all of them is eggs, to which different fillings are added. The combinations of fillings are almost endless. There is chicken kuku, garlic kuku, eggplant kuku, yogurt kuku, and lima bean kuku, to name just a few.

Seven Dishes

During No Rooz, Iranians set seven dishes each beginning with the letter S on the holiday table. Dishes beginning with this letter are considered lucky. Each dish represents an important aspect of life. Sabzeh (SOB zay), or sprouts, represent rebirth. Samanu (sah mah NEW), or wheat pudding, symbolizes growth. Sib (seeb), or apple, represents beauty. Serkeh (sayr KAY), or vinegar, symbolizes patience. Senjed (sen JED), or dried fruit, represents love. Somaq (so MAWG), or sumac berries, represent life. Finally, sir (seer), or garlic, symbolizes health.

Koofteh

Iranians like meatballs, which they call koofteh (koof TAY). These meatballs are not like American-style meatballs. Koofteh is made from a combination of ground lamb, rice, split peas, and herbs, which is formed into a paste and shaped into meatballs. Special foods are placed in the center of each meatball. Nuts, dried fruit, and hard-boiled eggs are common. But for special occasions a whole chicken may be placed inside. Typical Iranian meatballs are about the size of an orange, but they can be a lot larger depending on the stuffing.

But it is herb kuku that Iranians serve at celebrations.

This festive dish is made with eggs and lots of fresh herbs. Garlic, parsley, chives, cilantro, dill, and saffron are popular. The ingredients have special meaning for Iranians, which is one reason herb kuku is a New Year's favorite. The herbs symbolize the beginning of what Iranians hope will be an abundant growing season. The eggs, a traditional symbol of birth, promise No Rooz celebrators many children and grandchildren in the coming year.

In the past, cooks made herb kuku in an iron skillet set on hot coals. Coals were also placed on the lid of the pan to make sure both the top and the bottom of the kuku cooked evenly. Today, most cooks make herb kuku in an oven. To start, they mix eggs, baking powder, chopped herbs, and flour. At the same time, they melt butter and pour it into a baking pan. Then they pour the egg mixture into the pan and bake the kuku in the oven. It rises and takes on the shape of the baking pan. About ten minutes before the kuku is done, the cook pours melted butter over it. To make the kuku more festive, chopped walnuts and raisins are sprinkled on the

Herb Kuku

Herb kuku takes longer to make than a regular omelet, but it is worth the wait.

Ingredients:
6 eggs
pinch each of salt, pepper, and cinnamon
2 teaspoons flour
1 teaspoon baking powder
1 cup green onions, chopped
1 cup parsley, chopped
1 cup cilantro, chopped
3 tablespoons butter
handful of raisins or walnuts (optional)

Instructions:
1. Preheat the oven to 350° F.
2. Break the eggs into a large bowl. Add salt, pepper, and cinnamon, and mix. Add the flour, baking powder, and chopped herbs. Mix well.
3. Melt the butter in a baking dish. Pour the egg mixture on top and bake until the kuku is brown on top, about 45 minutes.
4. Sprinkle a handful of raisins or walnuts on top before serving, if desired.

Serves 4–6

A sunny day brings an Iranian family outside for a picnic.

top. With its soft green center, crisp bottom, and light golden brown top, herb kuku is a taste treat. It is, according to Ramazani, "the finest and most delectable of all the kookoos [kukus]"[16]

Special Picnics

It is not only its symbolic ingredients and great taste that makes herb kuku a No Rooz favorite. Iranians typically eat herb kuku on the thirteenth day of No Rooz, which, according to Iranian tradition, is spent outdoors. Families head to the country, where they have picnics. Because herb kuku tastes just as good cold as it does hot, it is found in almost every picnic basket. "Iranian families leave their homes on that morning with carpets, . . . and picnic materials to search out gardens and areas beside streams and under trees," explains an article on Iranian Hotline, a Web site dedicated to all things Iranian. "At noon," the article continues, "each family spreads out its food and all eat a substantial soup, there is green herb pilaf, fried fish and kuku, a fried omelet-like dish thick with chopped greens."[17]

Herb kuku is also popular during **Ramadan** (RAHM-ah-dahn). During this monthlong religious holiday, Muslim people fast from dawn to dusk. But each evening when the fasting ends, they feast. Herb kuku is a traditional fast breaker. After a day without food, its lightness makes it easy to digest. And because it tastes so good, it is a perfect way to celebrate.

Diners enjoy good food and good company at an upscale Tehran restaurant, where old and new traditions mix in a uniquely Iranian style.

Whether eating jeweled rice at weddings and banquets, savoring ajil during No Rooz, or breaking the Ramadan fast with herb kuku, Iranians love to celebrate. Special foods help make important occasions more memorable and fun.

Metric Conversions

Mass (weight)

1 ounce (oz.)	= 28.0 grams (g)
8 ounces	= 227.0 grams
1 pound (lb.) or 16 ounces	= 0.45 kilograms (kg)
2.2 pounds	= 1.0 kilogram

Liquid Volume

1 teaspoon (tsp.)	= 5.0 milliliters (ml)
1 tablespoon (tbsp.)	= 15.0 milliliters
1 fluid ounce (oz.)	= 30.0 milliliters
1 cup (c.)	= 240 milliliters
1 pint (pt.)	= 480 milliliters
1 quart (qt.)	= 0.95 liters (l)
1 gallon (gal.)	= 3.80 liters

Pan Sizes

8-inch cake pan	= 20 x 4-centimeter cake pan
9-inch cake pan	= 23 x 3.5-centimeter cake pan
11 x 7-inch baking pan	= 28 x 18-centimeter baking pan
13 x 9-inch baking pan	= 32.5 x 23-centimeter baking pan
9 x 5-inch loaf pan	= 23 x 13-centimeter loaf pan
2-quart casserole	= 2-liter casserole

Temperature

212° F	= 100° C (boiling point of water)
225° F	= 110° C
250° F	= 120° C
275° F	= 135° C
300° F	= 150° C
325° F	= 160° C
350° F	= 180° C
375° F	= 190° C
400° F	= 200° C

Length

1/4 inch (in.)	= 0.6 centimeters (cm)
1/2 inch	= 1.25 centimeters
1 inch	= 2.5 centimeters

Notes

Chapter 1: Ancient Ingredients

1. *Persian Mirror,* "Persian Cuisine Basic Tastes," www.persian mirror.com/cuisine/intro/intro.cfm.

2. Margaret Shaida, *The Legendary Cuisine of Persia.* New York: Interlink, 2000, p. 53.

3. Shaida, *The Legendary Cuisine of Persia,* p. 10.

4. Iran Tour, "Iranian Foods," www.irantour.org/Iran/food/Desserts.html.

5. Nesta Ramazani, *Persian Cooking: A Table of Exotic Delights.* Bethesda, MD: Ibex, 2000, p. 139.

Chapter 2: Welcoming Dishes

6. Shaida, *The Legendary Cuisine of Persia,* p. 97.

7. Najmieh Batmanglij, *New Food of Life: Ancient Persian and Modern Iranian Cooking and Ceremonies.* Washington, DC: Mage, 2005, p. 51.

8. Setareh Sabety, "Simple Yet Noble Piece of Heritage," *Iranian,* January 11, 2002. www.iranian.com/SetarehSabety/2002/January/Chelo/index.html.

Chapter 3: Afternoon Treats

9. Hamid Taghavi, "*eid-didany* = Eat 'Til You're Beat," *Iranian,* March 16, 1998. www.iranian.com/Satire/March98/Traditions/index.html.

10. Ramazani, *Persian Cooking,* p. 220.

11. Quoted in Shaida, *The Legendary Cuisine of Persia,* p. 238.

12. Shaida, *The Legendary Cuisine of Persia,* pp. 236, 238.

13. Salam Iran, "Food & Drinks," www.salamiran.org/CT/Tourism/food_and_drinks.html.

Chapter 4: Special Foods for Special Occasions

14. Epicurious.com, "Jeweled Rice with Dried Fruits," www.epicurious.com/recipes/recipe_views/views/230733.

15. Shaida, *The Legendary Cuisine of Persia,* p. 16.

16. Ramazani, *Persian Cooking,* p. 55.

17. Iranian Hotline, "Norooz, The Iranian New Year," www.iranianhotline.com/Norooz.cfm.

Glossary

ab-goosht: An Iranian soup made with meat.

ajil: A mix of dried fruits, nuts, and seeds.

ash: A meatless Iranian soup.

baklava: A layered pastry filled with nuts and honey.

basmati rice: A fragrant type of rice.

chelow: Steamed rice used in almost every Iranian meal.

clarified butter: Butter from which all milk solids have been removed.

doogh: An Iranian drink made with yogurt and carbonated water.

Farsi: The language spoken in Iran.

fesenjan: A lamb stew made with pomegranate syrup, walnuts, onions, and cinnamon.

garnishes: Toppings added to decorate foods.

kebabs: Skewered meat that is roasted over charcoal.

khoresh: The Iranian word for stew.

kuku: An egg dish similar to an omelet.

marinates: Flavoring meat, poultry, or fish by soaking it in liquid before cooking it.

No Rooz: The Iranian New Year's celebration.

Persia: The name used for Iran from ancient times until the 20th century.

phyllo: A thin dough used to make baklava.

polow: Cooked rice mixed with vegetables, meat, and/or fruit.

Ramadan: A monthlong religious holiday during which Muslims fast from dawn to dusk.

saffron: A rare and expensive spice that comes from the crocus flower.

sharbat: An Iranian drink made from fruit syrup and crushed ice.

Silk Road: An overland route used by ancient traders between Europe and Asia that went through Iran.

tah dig: A crisp layer of rice that sticks to the bottom of the cooking pot.

For Further Exploration

Books

Diane Hoyt-Goldsmith, *Celebrating Ramadan*. New York: Holiday House, 2001. This books uses photographs to look at Ramadan and how it is celebrated.

Kerena Marchant, *Muslim Festival Tales*. Austin, TX: Raintree Steck-Vaughn, 2001. In this book, Muslim festivals are depicted through songs, poems, plays, and recipes.

Don Nardo, *Ancient Persia*. San Diego, CA: Blackbirch, 2004. Readers learn about daily life in ancient Persia.

Joanne Richter, *Iran, the Culture*. New York: Crabtree, 2005. Life in modern Iran is the theme of this book.

Stacy Taus-Bolstad, *Iran in Pictures*. Minneapolis: Lerner, 2004. Readers look at the geography and daily life in Iran through pictures.

Web Sites

Global Kids, "Around the World with Humpty Dumpty" (www.globalkids.info/v3/index.cfm?oid=search&contentsearch=Persia&aroundhumpty=yes). Information just for kids about Iran, including facts, national holidays, maps, Persian stories, and fairy tales.

History for Kids, "The Persians" (www.historyforkids. org/learn/westasia/history/persians.htm). This site contains a wealth of information on ancient Persia.

Iran Mania, "Persian Cooking" (www.iranmania.com/ travel/eating). This Web site has lots of Iranian recipes.

Index

abdugh (doogh), 40
ab-ghoosht (lamb broth), 22
ajil, 44–47
almonds, 30–31, 41
ash (soup), 21–22
Assyria, 29

baklava, 28–32
basmati rice, 4, 6
Batmanglij, Najmieh, 21
beef, 10
beverages, 33
  doogh, 38–40
  sharbat, 34–38
  tea, 35, 36
broth, 22

celebration foods
  ajil, 44–47
  herb kuku, 47–49, 51
  jeweled rice, 41–44
  seven "s" dishes, 47
chelow, 7, 8–10, 14
chicken, 42
cookies, 32–33, 36

dining customs, 25
doogh, 38–40
dried fruits
  in history, 11, 13
  for No Rooz, 44–45
  for snacks, 15
drinks. See beverages
eggs, 48
Epicurious.com (Web site), 44

Farsi, 44
fesenjan, 14–15
flowers, edible, 14
fruit
  dried, 11, 13, 15, 44–45
fresh fruit cocktail, 12
  in history, 11
  lamb and, 10, 14–15
  in sharbat, 34, 36, 37
  in soup, 22
ghormeh sabzi (herb khoresh), 19
good luck, 45–47

green beans, 18

health
  promise soup and, 21
  sharbat for, 37–38
  symbol of, 47
herb khoresh, 19
herb kuku, 47–49, 51
Herodotus, 33
hospitality, 16, 36

Iranian Hotline (Web site), 51

jeweled rice, 41–44

kebabs, 23–27
khoresh (stews), 16, 18–21
King of Iranian dishes, 41–44
koofteh (meatballs), 48
kukus, 47–49, 51

lamb
  bones for broth, 22
  fruit and, 14–15

kebabs, 23–27
in khoresh, 19
in koofteh, 48
popularity of, 10–11
limes, dried, 15
lucky seven, 45–47

meat, 10
  see also lamb
meatballs, 48
milk, 35, 38
Muslims, 10

national dish, 23
No Rooz (New Year's celebration)
  ajil for, 44–47
  kukus for, 47–49, 51
nuts
  in baklava, 30–33
  in jeweled rice, 41
  for No Rooz, 44, 45

onions
  in kebabs, 26
  in soup, 22
  in stews, 18, 19–20

pastries, 28–32
Persia, 4, 29, 32–33
Persian Mirror (Internet magazine), 7

phyllo dough, 29
picnics, special, 51
pistachios, 30–31, 41
polow, 7
pomegranates, 14–15
pork, 10
promise soup, 21

Ramadan, 51
Ramazani, Nesta
  on baklava, 31–32
  on fesenjan, 15
  on herb kuku, 51
recipes
  ajil, 44
  chelow, 9
  doogh, 39
  fresh fruit cocktail, 12
  herb kuku, 49
  khoresh with green beans, 18
  lamb kebabs, 26
  walnut cookies, 32
rhubarb khoresh, 19
rice
  basmati, 4, 6
  choosing, 6–7
  cooking, 7–10
  importance of, 4
  jeweled, 41–44
rose petals, 14, 42
rosewater, 14, 34, 36

Sabety, Setareh, 27
sabzeh, 47
saffron, 8, 42
Salam Iran (Web site), 39–40
samanu, 47
samovars, 35
senjed, 47
serkeh, 47
Shaida, Margaret
  on ajil, 45
  on chelow, 10
  on herb khoresh, 19
  on lamb, 10–11
sharbat, 34–37
sheep, raising, 10
sherbet, 36
sib, 47
Silk Road, 4
sir, 47
slushes, 34
snacks
  baklava, 28–32
  cookies, 32–33, 36
  dried limes, 15
  rosewater ice cream and ices, 14
  sharbat, 34–37
snow cones, 34
sofrehs (tablecloths), 25
soft drinks, 38–40
somaq, 47
sorbet, 36

soups, 21–22
spices, 8, 42
stews, 16, 18–21
sugar
  in baking, 32–33
  spun, 43
  with tea, 35
Taghavi, Hamid,
  28

tah dig, 7, 8
Tahmasp (shah),
  34–35
tea, 35, 36
treats. *See* snacks

vegetables
  in kebabs, 26
  in soup, 22

in stews, 18,
  19–20

walnuts, 32
weddings, 42–43

Xenophon, 11

yogurt, 38–40

Picture Credits

About the Author

Barbara Sheen is the author of numerous works of fiction and nonfiction for young people. She lives in New Mexico with her family. In her spare time, she likes to swim, walk, garden, read and, of course, she loves to cook!